THE AFTERMATH: Chaos in the Age of Trump

BARBARIANS AT THE GATES

Poems of Resistance

Gregory Nelson Amour

ISBN:069206284X
ISBN-13:978-0692062845

DEDICATION

DEDICATED TO ALL WHO RESIST HATRED, BLIND IDEOLOGY (WHAT I TERM AS IDIOT-OLOGY), RACISM, DISCRIMINATION, DESTRUCTIVE TRIBALISM, OPPRESSION OF THE POOR, PURE PARTY POLITICS-WHATEVER THE COST, FANATICAL NATIONALISM, SELFISH GREED AND UNBRIDLED MATERIALISM, DISHONESTY-DISGUISED AS "ALTERNATE FACTS", AND WHO DREAM, WORK, FIGHT, AND TOIL FOR A MORE JUST NATION AND WORLD.

CONTENTS

ACKNOWLEDGMENTS

For all those who lead, fight and inspire the PEACEFUL, DETERMINED RESISTANCE: You have inspired me. This book is written as a poetic prophecy and account of an attempt to destroy the fabric and unity of our nation, and to inspire its resurrection to a more just, democratic society. It joins with all of you who long to awaken from a nightmare of lies, manipulations, and disregard for truth and decency. It joins with you to awaken to a dawn of hope, progress and justice toward all, that our children and grandchildren, and future generations can embrace and enshrine forever.

On the morning after election night, 2016, instead of awakening to a river of surging progress, we awakened to a:

POISONED WELL

Descending to the depths of darkness
Descending to the depths of hell
Wondering how it came to pass
We came to drink this poison well

Descending to the deep recession
Falling in the burning brine
Knowing that the bonds of hatred
Shackles hope, including mine

Praying for His ray of sunlight
Hoping for a holy sign
May God's rays of Love unite us
And make his healing power mine.

For too long of a 2016 campaign we heard bigoted comments, insults, race baiting, xenophobic comments, religious insults, and false promises and lies for those so desperate to hear them. With a great deal of interference from Russia, manipulation by WikiLeaks, throwing voters off the rolls, Republican suppression ID laws, and cynical racial and partisan gerrymandering, the nation was surprised at the result. It is as if Donald Trump, the Republican Party, the extreme nationalistic right wing, the Nazi Party and KKK all joined to barter the nation's soul for power. And so …

SATAN ARISES -SPIRITUAL INSURRECTION

Satan now arises from his gate

Transforming promised lies into hate

Those who embraced them repent too late

Satan lets lose the demons from his gate

They did this in the name of God

Crushing dispossessed into the sod

Fear and anger he knew how to prod

And beating all the "Others" with his rod

They took us to the nonexistent past

When persecution of "others" had been cast

By fears of creeds and colors for too long last

The unmade present burned into the remade past

God's Creation sullied, the earth was bled

Native peoples exploited til their land was dead

Hatred, Fear, Reprisal--the demons fed

Until God's compassion lies lifeless, our hearts now dead

The Holy Cross of Healing, now slowly bleeds

As Jesus weeps that in his name are planned cruel deeds

As Satan plants by race, religion, love choice, his divisive seeds

The crown of thorns struck deeper with woven reeds

All hail the rebirth of the Age of Greed

All hail the crushing down of those in need

The Christ is slain in his own name to bleed

What's done is done to all, divisive deed

So tell me, was Jesus truly white, or brown?

Again crucified, Alt-Right side up or upside down?

Take the flaming rod and strike his bleeding crown

And let the Dreamers dreams in hatred drown?

Pray the angels shout their spiritual insurrection

That we may choose his Love, his communal direction

And give the poor, the immigrant, the "others" His protection

And wait, for His return, His amnesty, His Love and Resurrection.

The absurd campaign rhetoric, the rowdy red meat rallies, the insults of other candidates, the simplistic slogans, the impossible promises were accepted by enough (THOUGH NOT THE MAJORITY OF) voters and resulted in the unthinkable nightmare of a wannabe dictator, joined by right wing zealots, ideological extremists, and racial and religious bigots. They were intent on destroying everything they envied, feared, and resented. Seeing the City on the Hill, they became:

BARBARIANS AT THE GATES (Inauguration 2017)

Barbarians at the City Gates

Riding in on Fear and mongered Hate

Polluting water, earth and air

So Greed and Power, kings and lords can share

Barbarians tearing down the City Wall

All civil progress their aim to stall

The ruins, blocks of ivory and marbled stone

Smashed apart so each a part can own

Vandals at the City Shrine

"What once was yours," they say. "is mine."

Changing the values of Truth we hold

Into tarnished silver and corrupted gold

Mockers at the Statue's Door

Keep out the "wretched, the tired, the poor"

Extinguish the Lantern of hope once flaming bright

The burning City Is their demented light

Foul the air with charred fossil smell

Fresh air we breathed, now a lying tale

Water filled with debris and burning trash

Brings polluting hordes, polluted cash

Houses seized with another lie

They rejoice as the indigent freeze and die

The spoils for 30 pieces of silver trade

As they laugh at the populace now betrayed

Children, elders, disabled struck down

The immigrant cast back into the river to drown

The sick reduced to begging for care

This, the result of the lord's greedy lair

Coins of silver and fools' foolish gold

Dazzled some eyes, who now in servitude sold

Gatekeepers betrayed the City for a lie

They too will be betrayed and decreed to die

Resist, Resist the Barbaric Hordes

Never bend to or praise the looting lords

One day a rebuilt City will shine

What once was theirs, will again be "yours and mine."

Why did so many Americans allow themselves to be so bamboozled into thinking that Nihilism and negativity, anger and lashing out blindly would make the nation "Great Again?" Is it the same reason that an angered child cries out in absurd tantrums? Or, a selfish desire to get a piece of the pie they believe "others" (disregard the top 5%) are taking away to make them want to shout :

I’ve got Mine (America Great Again :Satire)

I’ve got mine

Don’t care about theirs

Got my ladder

Collapse their stairs

Take away their land

I’ve got mine

Let them drink mud

I’ll drink my wine

I’vc got my health

Let them be sick

Cheaper not to treat them

Let death do its trick

I’ve got my family

Tear theirs apart

I’ve got my money

Who needs heart

I’ve got my freedom

Take theirs away

Make the “Others” go

All “My Kind” can stay

I fly through clouds

They can crawl through slime

Take them away

I’ve got mine.

Over and over we heard the all too common paranoid, manipulative cry of all fascist leaders, THE GREAT I will make the nation and all of you "Great Again!" And how do they do this? They look for scapegoats. And so they join in demagoguery to blame "The Others." The other races, the other religions, the other countries, the other belief systems, the other political parties, the other immigrants,...the demonic "Others." By banning, demonizing, attacking, hating, "The Other," the manipulators claim they will make the nation great again. This is the oldest claim made by all potential dictators and tyrants. "Give me your TOTAL trust and loyalty and " I and I alone" will make you great! Mussolini, Franco, Hitler, Stalin, and. Yes, Donald's good friend, Putin, dictators all, taught the extreme right wing too well by example, how to corrupt a democracy from the inside to eventually destroy it. It is a simple process to blame and demonize "The Others." This was the formula used to inject venom, anger, hate, and irrational passion by Bannon, Trump, the alt-Right, Extreme Right Wing, and its "Religious" allies. It was a knowing farce filled with fake information, lies, demonizing and false promises to make America:

Great Again -- Fascism's Rhapsody(Satire)

I have my God

He's on my side

"Do unto others"

Need not abide

My God is white

Not black or brown

If I'm gonna be up

Gotta keep you down

My God's for me

Doesn't care about you

Only my prayers are heard

Nothing you can do

Cause I am richer

God loves me best

If you are poorer

You don't pass his test

You got to be wrong

Cause I'm always right

I'm gonna be "Great Again"

Cause my God is white.

So, in the Puritanical Tradition of witch hunting, at rallies and campaign events, the most rabid of the Trump supporters asked themselves, “Who shall be the first witches to burn?” Of course the easiest answers were the “immigrants.” It did not matter that Congress, for over thirty years refused to take up the issue. It did not matter that though several solutions were proposed, Congressional Republicans blocked and stalled every one.

It did not matter that we opened the gates when we needed farm laborers to pick the crops that we eat , or wash the clothes we wear, or wash the dishes from which we eat, or pick our weeds, or care for our children, or nurse and bathe our elderly and sick. It did not matter that children were brought here and lived here most of their lives as the only country they knew. It didn’t matter if they came here to escape violence and wars, often caused by U.S. intervention into their own nation’s politics. It did not matter, case by case, what would be a just solution. It was easier to brand all as “criminals” and “lawbreakers” and “rapists”. They were immigrants fleeing into a promised land to find safety and refuge, and yes, sanctuary. Immigrants, fleeing for their lives or livelihood in the very same way that:

Jesus Came Into Our Midst

Jesus came into our midst

A child, poor and ignored

Not a king who possessed a crown

Or a tyrant needing to be adored

Jesus came to give his message

One of compassion and of love

While others lived in fear and hate

God of All blessed His words above

Jesus came as an immigrant

No home in which to live

A stable full of straw and earth

A welcome was all we had to give

His message was compassion and love
Not one of exclusion and hate
And if we should bar others from that love
We may be banned from heaven's gate

Be careful not to praise the powers
Who condemn the persecuted and poor
For how we treat "The least of these"
May ban us from heaven's door

Exclude and blame the immigrant
Who for years made this land their own
And we may find our eternal home on that
Last Day
The "First" Land of Burning Brine and
Stone.

(*"For you will be treated as you treat others. The standard you use in judging others is the standard by which you will be judged." Matthew, 7:2*)

In American history there have been several crimes we have swept under the rug so that we don't have to face, wrestle with, confess, repent, redeem and repair the harm and aftermath of historical policies that have devastated whole communities and races, Many still bear the scars of those historical crimes. Among those crimes are the sins of slavery and the genocide of Native Americans. Though we personally may not have participated in the actual commission of those original crimes, when we ignore, justify, mythologize, and perpetuate the harm that afflicts descendants of these communities, we open those wounds and scars. Some of the most powerful "leaders" sit like Pontius Pilate and pretend to wash their hands of harm caused by their policies, propaganda, legislation or executive orders. And their supporters and enablers are like the rabble outside the palace balcony who cry:"Their blood be on us and on our children." And for generation after American generation, it is. And as long as that cry is repeated in spirit and the sins of the past are not repaired, it presents the sins from being forgiven, healed, or redeemed. For many of those sins were committed:

In God's Name

Columbus explored America. Columbus searched for Gold
His ruthless enslavement of Natives is a story that has been told

Some hail him as a hero: Fairy tales and altered history can be nice to tell
Yet the Natives he decimated claim he is the cause of their death knell

How many hands did he cut off if not enough gold to fill?
How many did he whip and enslave? How many did he kill?

To some he was a hero who enriched their power and their purse
To his victims he brought pain and greed, and a genocidal curse

No need to praise explorers who searched for power gold and fame
But weep and pray for those they killed for gold and in God's name.

With short memory of history and the same sense of power, money and greed, oil barons, banks, and immoral politicians continued a modern form of moral, spiritual, economic, and physical genocide.

Observe the executive order of Trump ,who, accepting and approving the greed of oil companies, bankers, and investors, ordered the opening of Standing Rock to drilling, pollution and desecration of historical Indian land. The dangers of polluting nearby waters from which the people and their children drink were ignored. The desecration of graveyards and sacred lands were mocked. Peaceful protesters were cruelly beaten and hosed in freezing weather. Mark this a modern continuation of Genocide of the American Indian. It is a case of oil over decency, money over spiritual right, racism over justice. Thus, the Native American Genocide continues in yet another sinister way. To add to this shame, Trump tried to illegally rescind and reduce Bears Ears National Monument, another Shrine of Native Heritage, by over 85%. Additionally, that same discriminatory order aimed to reduce Grand Staircase-Escalante National Monument by 45%. And throughout our petitions, prayers, protests, law suits, and National Shame over this new atrocity, all we can now do is stain the shame of

Trump and those who support this sin, by offering our:

TEARS FOR STANDING ROCK (Executive Order)

They Profane their age old Sacred Land

They Defile Their graves and Holy Sites

They do this because they are "humble Reds"

And Power belongs to Billionaire Whites.

Those who commit these new sins against Native Americans and their historical Lands must remember God's commandments and promises toward those who harbor injustice to the weak and dispossessed.

"Thou shall not steal!" and

"Vengeance is mine says the Lord . I will pay them back, I promise."

From 2006 on, and through the Trump Regime of 2017 the Republican led Do Nothing Congress wasted its time attempting multiple times to dismantle Obamacare. That program saved thousand of lives and provided an additional 20 million Americans with health insurance coverage they could not otherwise afford. By requiring most Americans to be insured, it made possible for many more Americans to be able to have affordable, quality health care insurance with subsidies for those who could not otherwise get coverage. Single parents, children, the working poor and the impoverished could now have the right to attend to their health in a proactive and humane manner. Prior to Obamacare legislation, millions were one sickness away from losing their homes, and lives from expensive or inadequate care.

The Republican members of Congress, and many of their supporters, found this acceptable and preferable to human and Christian values accepted as rights in every democratic Western country, except, shamefully, the United States. Once attaining a majority, the Republican led Congress waged war on the growing number of Americans who, otherwise, could not afford and did not have health coverage for themselves, their families and their children. This included older Americans whose premiums were too expensive and those with prior conditions, who could not get coverage. Many lost coverage, though previously insured, once they were diagnosed with an ongoing expensive condition.

Though Obamacare repaired these inequities, Republicans in Congress and in governorships throughout the states, with a few courageous exceptions, did everything they could to challenge, dismantle, attack and sabotage a program which became overwhelmingly approved by Democrats and Republican and Independent citizens alike. But, hatred is hatred, Whether prompted by an outdated anti-government philosophy, or mean spirited arrogance that only the wealthy should have insurance, a slap in the face to tax payers who subsidize Congressional members' own insurance, (the best and most expensive there is) or a cheap right wing revolt against everything Obama tried to do for the American people, they closed their hearts. Sickness has no prejudices and attacks all indiscriminately. The Republican congress prior to, and especially during the regime of Trump , sounded the cry of the :

PHARISEES AND HYPOCRITES

Ye Pharisees and Hypocrites

You have a log stuck in your eye

You mock the sick and working poor

Turn aside to lose their health and die

The hypocritical attacks were attempted again, during Trump's habitation of the White House, and in the face of his LIES that they would “improve” Obamacare. They came up with new efforts to destroy a program that the MAJORITY of Americans demanded to be kept. Indeed, they created a mockery of a non plan that had nothing but destruction of that MAJORITY APPROVED reform Americans came to like, approve and trust. The Republican House voted to destroy the program: “Damn the American people!” The Republican Senate had only three courageous members who saved the basic program. Later, Trump promised to sabotage it and let it die The failed Non- Plan was called:

TRUMPCARE: THE REPUBLICAN PLAN--(Satire)

Rejoice! Rejoice

The poor have lost their muted voice

The Great America now I see

Where all the best belongs to me

Destroy! Destroy!

Their health--a cast off toy

So hard I try and try and try

To believe our self-made selfish Lie

Deny all balanced human scope

To take away their desperate hope

Lie and scheme and take without a hitch

More tax breaks for the Greedy Rich

Let the mothers and fathers die

Who cares if others' children cry

As long as I get my selfish own

I'll be the "First" to cast my stone

Give them FAKE "access" and Rejoice!

For I know lack of money gives no choice

So let the others' children cry

Cheaper to let their parents die

The wealthiest get the best that's there

No choice for poor cause we don't care

If others have some greater need

Just laugh at them and let them bleed

Remember the words of God on High

When on our bed as we prepare to die

"They who deafen ears to the cries of the poor

Will be heard by God on High no more".

("They who close their ears to the cries of the poor will themselves cry out and not be heard." The Book Of Proverbs)

Throughout the first chaotic Trumpian year, the leaders of the Republican dominated Congress accomplished nothing. They did, however, collude and scheme with Donald Trump on how to coddle the wealthy and cudgel the middle and working class, working poor, and indigent. In the last month of Trump's first year regime, there was a desperate rush to give Trump and their Corporate pimps their demanded booty. In 28 secretive, desperate, chaotic days, the GOP Congress created a series of tax schemes that essentially gave the wealthiest of Americans and their Corporate pimps nearly 2 Trillion dollars at the expense of every program and benefit the middle class, their children and seniors depended on. Though the majority of Americans overwhelmingly opposed this legislation, the Republican Congress bowed to their masters and delivered a lie to the American people. There were no hearings. There were no interviews with experts. There was no credible data to back up their magic claims that somehow all the debt that would burden another generation would pay for itself. But, just in case, they would include another sabotage of Obamacare, and vowed to attack Social Security and Medicare. To make the top 5% wealthier, the victims would be education, children, seniors, health care for the elderly, health care for the poor and homeless. But, that is what Barbarians do! Thus, the Corporate Pimps and Billionaires, like Trump and friends, were successful in calling in their payments from the Republican members of congress who acted as their Political Whores who screwed…no, Raped the working classes, and extracted money to pay to their baron pimps. And so through lies, schemes, denied debt and arrogant rejection of the will of the Majority of Americans they, on a pure tribal

Party line vote, forced on Americans the:

TRUMP TAX and BUDGET SCAM

To pass "Tax Reform": This is the test

Give the Billionaires the very best

Increase your tax to build a wall?

Upon our pockets the expense would fall

The Budget scam will pass the test

If in it Billionaires can invest

In a tax that falls most on we who need

So that it is OUR children left to pay and bleed

Tax deductions to buy that "Office Yacht"

School children eat? "No they may not!"

Who runs this divided nation now?

Not those of us who pull the plow

But our corporate lawyers and CEOs

Wealth and power for these few grows

This ‘budget” from hearts both cruel and cold
Toward workers, children, sick, poor and old
Stamp out programs that help those in need
In favor of power with unbounded greed

Scandals, lies, his own Fake News
Right wing racist, fascist views
Half baked plans and baseless boasts
And luxury, greed filled, champagne toasts

Months and months of childish tweets
Failed bills and empty inauguration seats
Ego, boasts and his crazy brain
Can never make us “Great Again.”

In the midst of the chaos and the attempt by Trump, Bannon, Miller, Gorka, and right wing allies to totally disrupt the Democracy America fought so hard to attain, there was the destabilizing name calling, hate baiting, immigrant bashing and propagandizing of the Trumpian Right Wing. While so called decent supporters of Trump stood by in enabling silence, the propagators of division and hate came together to wave their Torches of Hate and scream their slogans of racism. Reminiscent of the brown shirts of Nazi Germany and the Post Bellum Ku Klux Klan, these mostly white, paranoid, insecure males sought to resurrect a period of racist hate and white dominance that caused a civil war here at home and a world war seven decades ago. They joined their fuehrer, Donald Trump, in decrying the right of local communities to decide where to put their outdated statues in response to the majority of those cities' residents. The residents and elected representatives of these cities saw these statues as outdated remnants of an era which celebrated slavery, discrimination, segregation and wholesale injustice towards black Americans and people of color. To resurrect an age of injustice, hate and white superiority, these troubadours of hate gathered to sing:

SATAN'S SIREN SONG : " ALT-RIGHT"

Like Cockroaches that spread out at Night

And scatter when exposed to Light

Hordes of Hate laying wait in the Dark

Awaiting Devil's Hate let lose by hate speech spark

Claiming Satan's Hate that makes them Right

Boiling up from Hell, once out of sight

Spreading Hate and Violence across the land

Raising Nazi Salutes and Slavery Flags with Fascist Hand

Like Carrion of Dead Carcass they lay in wait

To spread their vile, Godless, Divisive Hate

Rejecting Love and Justice, Compassion and Light

The Siren Song of Satan's Spawn: the sick Alt-Right

Note: Paraphrasing from Lutheran pastor Martin Niemoller:

First they came for the Jews, and I said nothing. Then they came for the intellectuals and I said nothing. Then they came for gays, and I said nothing, then they came for those who spoke out, so I said nothing ,,,AND THEN THEY CAME FOR ME!

Meanwhile, there had been very little public objection to the national Chaos by the Republicans in the House of Representatives. The lingering call to do something…anything to give the Republican Trump regime some claim of accomplishment and save the Republican controlled Congress from its utter failure, an all out war against the middle and working Class took place. The Tax Scam was not liked or supported by the majority of Americans. A meager few Republican senators spoke up, at first, but as the end of the first Trumpian year approached, the all too few voices of conscience, descended into a roaring lull of silence and acquiescence. "Oh well, we'll fix that later." By the time the Tax Scam was passed and far right extreme judges were rushed through with changed Senate rules and little testimony and debate, Republican promises of fairness and legitimacy of the process turned into deference and lies. "Power at any price," seemed to be their psychic mantra. And that price was the sanctity of the legislative process, the concern for fair play, working America, and the good of the country. In its place a quick, cheap power play for the short term optics for the party and the greed for power. In the line of right wing Congressional sites were schemes to dismantle Social Security, Reduce Medicare, Medicaid, Disability protections, educational programs, veteran benefits, and have the working classes get less from government while setting them up to pay more for the Congressional Gift to the Wealthiest 5% of Americans. This included benefits for the Billionaire-in-Chief. They delivered to their corporate and billionaire pimps the money paid for their souls. The political prostitutes not only watched as the children of the working class were mugged, but by the end of that disastrous do nothing 114th Congress, they handed the Mugger-in Chief a bigger club, and then proceeded to join in the Mugging themselves. They too joined, and became the Barbarians at the City Gates,

"Health-care? "Let the poor pay and die." Help for

college? “Our own children go, why should we provide the opportunity for others?”

Expand medicare? “We have the best tax payer subsidized insurance, so raid the health of the elderly to pay our Billionaire pimps.”

Protections for clean water for our children? Clean air for our children to breathe? National park protections for generations of our offspring to preserve? Gun safety? In the words of the favorite hero of our Colluder-in Chief, “Nyet, Nyet, Nyet!”

This 114th Republican Congress, as several Republican Congresses before it has a legacy that the Speaker of the House, [illegible] Ryan’s children can one day bc ashamed of, as can the grandchildren of Senatc Leader Mitch McConnell. It is being recorded in history as a Spineless Enabler of Executive Obstruction, Overreach, Corruption, and yes, Collusion. The 114th and 115th Congresses will be known as the:

Cold Stone Congress (114th and 115th GOP)

Their heads are like bricks

Their hearts are like Stone

Give all to the Rich

Leave the sick and poor alone

Their soul is like Stone

Their hearts are like bricks

To the wealthy they give Gold

To the rest, derisive kicks

Their hearts are like bricks

Their souls made of Stone

The wealthy get more Steak

The rest are thrown the bone

By accepting and enabling the White House Chaos the Republican led congress, in effect, added to the anxiety of the country. A separate legislative branch of government was meant to advise, balance and check any out of control Executive branch. Instead, the Republican leaders and members of the 114th and 115th Congresses closed their eyes to the misdeeds of the Trump White House. By the end of the 2017 and the beginning of the new session in January 2018, the 114th and 115th Republican led congresses did more than enable the chaotic administration, they colluded with it to undermine the reputation, and thus, investigation of Special Consul Mueller and the integrity of the FBI. They insisted on going after Trump's political opponent, Hillary Clinton--a tactic employed by Vladimir Putin, against his political opponents. The paranoia of Trump and right wing of the party, infected the Republican Congress which seemed to have caught the disease of deception, and diversion; perhaps even obstruction.

The House investigation was waylaid and sabotaged by David Nunes, Trump's "Congressional Puppet." That title would be shared by   Ryan and Mitch McConnel. Instead of strengthening the nation and programs that served Americans, they became political prostitutes to Corporate and Billionaire Pimps. The 114th and 115th Congresses are being recorded in history as a Spineless Enabler of Executive Obstruction, Overreach, Corruption, and yes, Collusion.

And for the 30 pieces of silver paid by lobbyists and billionaires, they betrayed the trust of the American people, the morality and ethics of Jesus, and the flaunting of the warnings of the Prophets of Justice:

Remember The Prophets of Justice

Beware the God of Justice

Whom you claim to have adored

Remember his Divine Promise

" Vengeance is Mine, says the Lord."

Beware when you oppress his children

Beware when you abuse the poor

When His kingdom comes to fruition

Upon you he may close His door

Beware the God of Mercy

Should you violate his Love

The war waged against Justice

Will earn His Ire from above

Beware the God of Compassion

Who abhors all unjust laws

When He sees exclusion and repression

He sends punishments to give us pause

Beware the God of Vengeance

When his daughters and sons he sees you mock

When the Day of Judgment arises

Sins of hate weigh like a massive rock

Beware the God of Creation

When you tear up and pollute His Land

When you disrespect His Environment

Nowhere safe that you can stand

Beware the God of Justice

The Lord you claim to have adored

Remember forever His Promise

"I will pay the back. I promise, Says the Lord."

Those with a conscience, with a soul, with a spirit of justice, and human compassion have to ask: "What about the Homeless who will have their vulnerable survival threatened by reduced and gutted programs?What about the poorest children who will be deprived of school lunches and food programs? What about single working mothers who can barely feed and pay rent despite working two or three jobs? What about rural families who cannot afford adequate health insurance? What about elderly Americans who depend on social security, into which they have paid forty or fifty years or more? What about health insurance provided by Medicare into which elderly Americans pay and have paid for forty, fifty plus years, now under attack to pay for Billionaire tax cuts? What about family farmers who will suffer economic loss due to the attacks on food stamps programs, deported farm workers, and trade agreements with groups of nations, now abrogated? What about our families and children who are now expected to drink contaminated water, and breathe polluted air due to roll back of clean water and air protections? What about the poorest of the poor under assault by immoral actions of the Trump bureaucracy and the brutal acquiescence of an unethical, ungodly, greedy, obsequious Congress? The 114th and 115th Republican Congresses have closed their eyes and souls to the he plight of so many Americans. They have replaced concern for unity of the nation and finding bipartisan solutions to problems, with partisan tribalism and idiotic small minded outdated ideologies.

The 114th and 115th Republican Congresses, like the recent Republican led congresses before them, have abandoned the sacredness of the legislative process along with concern for decency and Justice for the poor and working classes. Not only have they betrayed the dignity of the Legislative branch, they have scorned, mocked, taunted and beaten Jesus and the Prophets of Justice. In their policies and enabling of Trumpian destruction, they have committed the act of:

Congressional Crucifixion (GOP)

They bargain with the devil

Trading power for their soul

Ignoring decrees of Heaven

For selfish bargains from Below

Mocking plights of the most needy

Ignoring those with endangered health

They bow down to praise the Greedy

Trade compassion for Gold and Wealth

Through Satanic chaos, in their silence and their Fear

They pretend they've never seen or ever heard

Cries for compassion or the need to shed a tear

Crucifying Jesus in the Others, they disobey His Word

Like Roman Soldiers, they laugh and slap His Face

With thorns they crown his Bleeding Head

To the chanting applause of their crucifying base

Then hang the Words of Justice on a Cross til it is dead

But will come that Final Moment, when they close their eyes in dread

They shall look into the mirror and hear all whom they despise

Cry out to Him for justice as they remember what He said

A Trumpet blows for justice, and with vengeance, Justice will Arise!

("Vengeance is mine says the Lord. I will pay them back. I promise." Deuteronomy)

The Republican Party and its financial backers have long had a love affair with the NRA. To be more direct, it has served as a Political Prostitute Ring for a rabid organization which profits from every bullet that tears into a child's flesh. It profits from every gun used to kill a police officer, every bump stock attached to a weapon to increase its killing potential, and by every spray of hundreds or thousands of bullets into unsuspecting crowds in which you and your loved ones may be a part. It profits from guns sold to gangs and terrorists, including right wing Nazis and KKK members, among others. It profits from a black market which smuggles guns to violent drug rings and gangs here and in Mexico, South America and overseas. It profits from death. For every death caused by a person wielding it, money has been exchanged for that weapon. For every box of bullets designed to kill a person, whether used to kill one, or hundreds, money had been exchanged for those bullets. In effect, dollars have been exchanged for lives. "Money, Money, Money.", 30 pieces of silver. And the Propaganda behind the exchange equals Death, Death, Death.

Let us be clear. There are no credible calls for taking away guns from law abiding households, from hunters, from sportsmen and women, and legitimate, licensed, responsible collectors. But there are no reasons for owning dozens of automatic and semi automatic weapons, and caches of thousands of bullets designed to kill human beings. A Majority of Americans believe that good and reasonable gun legislation is needed to restrict guns from those on terrorist watch lists, gang members, violent criminals, felons, spouse abusers, and mentally disturbed individuals with a history of proclivity toward violence.

Due primarily to Republican members of Congress, and yes, with some not so courageous, cowed Democrats, and their fear of NRA revenge and money in politics, we throw away thousands of lives a year and sweep the discussion and solutions under the rug. When the next massacres happen, they say it is not the time to discuss them, then hypocritically sweep "discussions" under the rug again: "Money, Money, Money."

Some divert the discussion to that of mental health issues and claim we need more programs. We do.

However, cynically, they never pony up the money for programs, and never get to real reasonable restrictions on gun violence.

We can count the massacres in our memories. There are too many memorials to the victims: children, mothers, sons, daughters, neighbors, and friends. I wager we all know someone who has been killed by a person wielding an all too accessible gun: Someone who shouldn't have had that gun in the first place.

NRA inspired Propagandists and unquestioning "Believers" expound that there should be no reasonable restrictions of guns as Propagation of Weapons is the intent of the Second Amendment. Wrong! That Amendment calls for guns in the hands of a "WELL REGULATED MILITIA," in a time when there was no national army and the newly proclaimed country was in danger of being attacked by its British overlords. Subsequently several Supreme Court decisions have upheld reasonable protections and restrictions on guns, Once again legislation has been pushed by NRA and Republican leaders to cash in on the Profiteers of Death. They reject all common sense solutions to an estimated 30,000 gun deaths a year, (34,000 gun deaths and 73,000 injuries in the U.S. were recorded in 2013 data).

Whose child, wife, husband, son, or daughter will be a victim next? Why are so many killed a year? Why so many deaths? Why so many high powered, automatic and semi automatic killing machines with easy access?

Many times a majority of Americans have raised these questions and called for a REAL discussion with SOLUTIONS by the legislature. However, the NRA and its manipulated cacophony of ideologues react against the instincts of common sense and the message of Christ: "Put down your weapon. He who lives by the sword, dies by the sword ." And die so many do.

In the place of common sense and intelligent discussion, there seems to be a cult of gun worship which seems so laughable and insane to the rest of the world. Like Pontius Pilate, most Republican legislators, along with some Democratic ones, hear the cries of the NRA Chief Priests and their clamoring groups, and attempt to wash their hands of any responsibility. " We wash our hands of this blood." And the NRA and the most rabid of the crowd raise their guns and say: "Their blood be on us and on our children" ...and it is. Too many times and too much blood on our children.

It is on the children of Sandy Hook, Rosenberg, and 292 other mass shootings in the last 274 days as of this writing. It is on the the children killed in the cities by gangs and drive -byes, and car to car and on children killed at school by other children, and suicide of our young , and in revenge killings: Guns, guns, guns everywhere…in the hands of the ones who should not have them. And the NRA and Republican legislature and Donald Trump wash their hands….but it does not wash their souls.

There is a False God in America. It is:

The God Of Guns

Hail to the God of Guns...
Assault weapons are its priests and nuns
Sacrifice is what the Gun God needs
He needs to see how humanity bleeds.

Worship the NRA if you please,
Raise your weapons and fall on your knees
The soul of a nation must we seize
Raise your Guns and fall on your knees

It is the God of Guns whom we must please...
Fire your weapons and fall on your knees
Violence is the nation's seed
Watch our children die and Bleed.

This is the Gun God's call we heed
We are baptized in the Gun God's need
Sacrifice our children and let them bleed.
To the Gun God's thirst, the Gun God's Greed!

A nation cannot be "Great Again" when the rest of the world laughs at its "leader," or distrusts it, or sees it lose its international leverage. Watching the Trump White House and its chaos has been like looking at a Tragedy. But, from another view, one could see its machinations, bumblings, inconsistencies, schemes, denials, lies, and idiocies as a Comedy, much as the outside world does. And so we have to see it from a point of view in which:

THINGS ONLY SILLY LIMERICKS CAN MAKE SENSE OF:

TINY TRUMP LIMERICK PACKET

There once was a LIAR named Trump

Who turned our environment into a dump

He said he had a GREAT plan

But it was just a GREAT SCAM

Soon all left of America will be a stump

There once was a VP named Pence

Who backed up things that make no sense

He supported lies that had no scope

When he defended lies of the Top Dope

So now his mouth and soul needs a rinse

There once was a Speaker named Ryan

Who his own guys said he's a lyin

He made a health care plan

That was nothing but spam

And Trump wanted his pants to be fryin

There once was a Committee Chair named Nunes, Dave

Who acted as Trumps personal slave

He sneaked to the White House after dark

Looking for a nonexistent spark

And now he is seen as the Idiot's Nave

There once was a liar named Kelly Ann

Who lied every way that she can

She gave laughable fake views

Called everything else Fake News

"Alternate Facts" was her only plan

There once was a Press secretary named Spicer

Who treated the facts like a Slicer

He stuttered and stammered

The truth was hacked and then hammered

And then he was sent to the dicer

There once was a schemer named Bannon

Who shot at Jews, blacks and Latins like a cannon

He hated everything not white

Loved hate, fascism and the Alt-Right

Now in trouble from just too much scammin

There once was a Tyrant named Putin

Who convinced Donny Boy to go lootin

"Do all the harm that you can"

"Put America in the can"

For Our Billionaire Control I'm a rootin"

And still there are the stubborn he can scam

Unthinking ones who support his evil plan

They're being used as his tool

And they look like a fool

Butting heads like a crazed, angry ram

Unfortunately, we must return back to the tragedy, a deep tragedy, happening every day within our communities. Trump, along with many of his right wing supporters, seems to have a real psychological problem with all kinds of immigration. Evidently, they must see the Statue of Liberty as a real affront to our nation; or not see it at all. They especially seem to have a problem of immigrants of color, immigrants who are poor, or of a different religion than their professed "Christianity."

The extreme right wing has always been a magnet for xenophobes, homophobes, misogynists, and racists. Trump's regime of White House immigrant bashers have brought their hatred for immigrants to a new cruel level. His Attorney General and Homeland Security Directors have transformed ICE(Immigration and Customs Enforcement) with new levels and tactics of intrusion, invasion, intimidation, violations of constitutional privacy, harassment, and bullying.

They have invaded churches, illegally entered homes without warrants, invaded workplaces without specific warrants, and even entered schools and school grounds to whisk away children from their parents and families. They have also taken away parents who waited to pick up their children from school. These tactics bring back the haunting memories of Nazi SS agents as they tore apart families as if they were cattle, instead of sacred human beings with families and loved ones, friends and neighbors. Their assault on these communities have been an assault on us all. If ICE agents have become despised under these new tactics, they, indeed, have earned it. There is no comfort for them here. Taking children from parents, schools and communities which are the only ones they know, and tearing parents from their children and families takes a certain kind of sinfulness deep with one's soul. Evil men cannot do evil deeds without their henchmen. Their henchmen cannot absolve themselves from sin. ICE agents are now the henchmen of an evil regime with evil, hurtful, inhumane and unchristian directives and policies.

"Oh, but the law must be followed!" , they say. Yes, the Nazi Germans said that too. The Chief Priest and Pharisees said that of Jesus. The slave holders said that. The defenders of Jim Crow laws exclaimed this. Segregationists said this. Indian land was stolen by laws. Native Americans were rounded up, massacred, and torn from their cultures because it was the law. Japanese Americans had their possessions taken and were sent to Internment "camps" because it was the law. Blacks were lynched in certain towns because it was once the law. People of color had to sit in the back of the bus and were denied use of "white only" restrooms because it was the law. Gays could be fired simply for being who they were and could not marry the one they loved and could be imprisoned because it was the law. Shameful "laws!" And shame came to all who enforced them, allowed them, promoted them, or ignored the consequences of their evil. The same is true today.

When laws that are immoral and evil are allowed to remain, the legislators and executives who ignore their evil and fail to fix them are immoral and evil. If a nation propagates, enacts, allows, and enforces laws that are inhumane and unjust, it too, is unjust. If laws are enforced in a cruel and inhumane way that causes undue harm, then that nation only dims the light of humanity. It is not "great" and can never be looked up to as a light among nations.

When families have been living in communities for many years, even decades, and have long been established and rooted in our neighborhoods, schools, churches, and workplaces, they have become part of the American fabric. Tearing that fabric apart tears at the heart and the soul and the mantle that once made the country great. For over 30 years the Republicans in Congress have catered to the xenophobes and blocked every attempt to fix a system almost all admit is broken. Several Republican and Democratic Presidents have sought Congressional fixes, to no avail. A vocal core of Republican legislators have refused their duty, with some courageous exceptions, and become part of that broken, inhumane, inexcusable system.

Hear the voice, not of the immigrant basher who refuses to heal the system, but rather that of a child who is sitting, waiting and hoping for her parents to return home as she finds herself:

Looking Out My Window: A Child's Storm

Cold, Cruel, Heartless

I look out the window

The Storm brings Destruction

The Storm Smashes

Tearing down what strives to grow

I see ICE

Children Torn Away in this Hateful Storm

Family Structures Torn Apart in this Hateful Storm

Neighborhoods that Belong

Workers that Belong,

Students that Belong

Families, friends, coworkers, neighbors that Belong

Torn by Cold, Cruel, Dividing Winds

Hateful Storm-- Hate inspired Storm

I see ICE

This Storm of Hate

This Cold Cruel Storm of Ignorance

This Terrible Cruel Storm that tears children away

A Storm that tears my brothers, my sisters away

That Hurricane of Hate that takes away my Mama, that

Disappears my Papa

That leaves me abandoned in a Flood of Fear

Full of Frigid, Frightful ICE

I Cry out to God for Mercy, I cry out to my neighbors for Mercy,

I cry out to my Family for help. Where are they?

I cry out to you.

Why do they not come home?

Is there no relief from this Storm?

It comes to my school.

It comes to my neighborhood.

It comes to my parks.

It comes to my home

It comes to my church.

Does it come for me?

Where is my Mama? Where is My Papa?

Where is my Sister and my Brother?

Taken Away by that Cold. Cruel, Hateful Storm

And all I see is … Cold… Cruel… Hateful …

ICE.

Suffice it to say we have been steeped in a time of political and personal chaos, hate filled rhetoric, and contradictory policies and directions. The option of someone totally morally, ethically, intellectually, spiritually and psychically unqualified to the highest office in the land has come back on this and future generations. It further aggravates the national crisis by having extremists, racists, extreme right wing ideologues (Idiot-ologists), propping up a totally unqualified leader and inflicting their agendas on the nation and on the world. Such enablers and supporters are in a delusional state when trying to bring back some non-existent past. So many long for some version of 1940s and 1950s when racism was legislated, when discrimination was the norm, when segregation was enforced, when xenophobia and homophobia were sanctioned and enshrined, when religious bigotry was preferred, when women were seen and treated as second class persons with limited options and rights to their own dignity and body, when it was men who decided how, when and why women would reproduce--a time when all the world was supposed to look like, think like, pray like, reproduce like ME. This is a time which never was. It is a time when only Hitlarian harm can result from fruitless attempts to make this Never-land of a society which never really existed an impossible reality. We know better! Never again!

The time has long passed when any institution, government, political party, corporation, religious institution, or institution of any kind can fantasize that they can forever control all the best for a few wealthy, privileged, powerful men. The times of injustice, however, need never return and must forever be challenged. They must never be allowed to take us backward. Unfortunately it is all too easy for Barbarians to set fire to the gates of a city and watch it burn. It is much harder to preserve the good and to build upon the foundations of justice and common sense and personal human dignity. These were the Foundations laid by the Fathers and Mothers of America, This was the goal and protection of the Constitution. Continuing to Build on those Foundations is the only way to repair the damage done by the Destroyers of Peace and Justice.

For now, we view the wreckage, with sadness, tears, and yes, anger, as well as resolve. And we record for all history, the Barbaric destruction that the Trumpian Regime, its Congressional enablers, and political supporters have rendered to our

Democracy as we view:

The Aftermath-- Age of Chaos

An age of chaos, a time of pain

Of hysterical tweets and corruption stain

Of oppressive hate and hate filled speech

Divisive rhetoric and bigotry they beseech

A time of Nazis and racist KKK

And Russian scandals that won't go away

Greed and money, scams and tricks

Sycophant Congress, hearts hard as bricks

A time of insults, attacks on the poor

On those who hope, just slam the door

Praise for dictators who obey no law

Alternative "truths" no one knew or saw

A time of selfishness, an age of lies

Racism and bigotry without disguise

Attacks on Courts and bigoted sin

A time that "made America small again".

We will, from this point on, continue to put out all the fires we can, and continue, with unceasing determination and commitment to defend every inch of the City on the Hill, our precious Constitutional Democracy.

Prepare to rebuild! After the assault is beaten back and collapses under its own weight of hatred, bigotry, injustice, mean spirited and ugly Ideology, we will have much to build. And build it better, more compassionate, more just and welcoming to all, we will!

Conquest Concluded

We will build our fortress, knock down that wall
Build Justice high and hold Truth tall
Construct a drawbridge, rebuild the gates
Throw out the hurts, destroy the hates

Rebuild the City, plant our fields
Pick up our spears, raise up our shields
No more surrender, no more fears
Our forests grow, we dry our tears

We laugh again: Our Cites Rejoice
We will applaud and raise our voice
Let lose the captives, free the dove
Spread Justice and replace their hate with Love.

Epilogue

I would like to thank those women and men who have inspired and motivated this book through their efforts to defend our decency and principles of an inclusive and democratic nation. They have proven that democracy can be attacked and undermined, but not defeated as long as good people speak up. Those who continue to support inclusive participation in our democracy, maximum participation in our elections, fair representation, and freedom of the press to hold the powerful accountable, are the present day heroes. They include millions of citizens united to make The United States a nation that can once again shine as that Just, Open, Diverse, Inclusive America: The Shining City on a Hill.

Among them: Special thanks to

Stephen Colbert
Seth Meyers
Anderson Cooper
Rachel Maddow
Oprah Winfrey
Ellen
Cast, Crew and Producers of Saturday Night Live
And so many others too numerous to mention
who stand in front of and protect against
The Barbarians At The Gates.

ABOUT THE AUTHOR

Gregory Amour has written and received remuneration for a TV Script, Sacred Identities, and produced, directed and acted in numerous stage plays. He has performed on local cable, and written scripts and presented voice narration on the topics of social justice and civil rights for public radio. He has written several hundred poems. Several of Gregory 's poems have been selected for and featured in anthologies of American Poetry, including Who's Who in Poetry, 2015. He currently has several video poems which have been produced on Youtube.

His passion for social justice, fair play, compassion, human dignity, and equal rights for all individuals can be seen in: The Aftermath: Chaos in the Age of Trump: Barbarians At The Gates: Poems of Resistance.

If you feel that this book can promote the cause of Justice and the preservation of our Democracy and Decency as a Nation, please consider sharing or giving this book to another. Or, perhaps a public official or representative. More copies can be ordered on Amazon.com You may also request your local book store to order a copy for you. Thank you for reading and your efforts to make the United Sates of America a better, more just, more inclusive nation: A Shining City on the Hill.

70077297R00044

Made in the USA
San Bernardino, CA
24 February 2018